D1385072

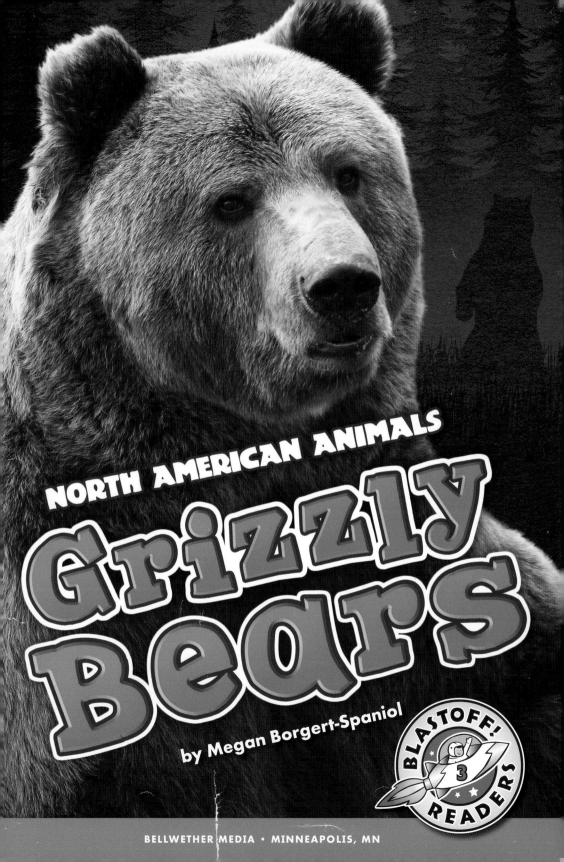

NORTH AMERICAN ANIMALS

Grizzly Bears

by Megan Borgert-Spaniol

BLASTOFF! READERS
3

BELLWETHER MEDIA • MINNEAPOLIS, MN

Note to Librarians, Teachers, and Parents:

Blastoff! Readers are carefully developed by literacy experts and combine standards-based content with developmentally appropriate text.

Level 1 provides the most support through repetition of high-frequency words, light text, predictable sentence patterns, and strong visual support.

Level 2 offers early readers a bit more challenge through varied simple sentences, increased text load, and less repetition of high-frequency words.

Level 3 advances early-fluent readers toward fluency through increased text and concept load, less reliance on visuals, longer sentences, and more literary language.

Level 4 builds reading stamina by providing more text per page, increased use of punctuation, greater variation in sentence patterns, and increasingly challenging vocabulary.

Level 5 encourages children to move from "learning to read" to "reading to learn" by providing even more text, varied writing styles, and less familiar topics.

Whichever book is right for your reader, Blastoff! Readers are the perfect books to build confidence and encourage a love of reading that will last a lifetime!

This edition first published in 2015 by Bellwether Media, Inc.

No part of this publication may be reproduced in whole or in part without written permission of the publisher. For information regarding permission, write to Bellwether Media, Inc., Attention: Permissions Department, 5357 Penn Avenue South, Minneapolis, MN 55419.

Library of Congress Cataloging-in-Publication Data

Borgert-Spaniol, Megan, 1989-
 Grizzly Bears / by Megan Borgert-Spaniol.
    pages cm. – (Blastoff! Readers. North American Animals)
 Includes bibliographical references and index.
 Summary: "Simple text and full-color photography introduce beginning readers to grizzly bears. Developed by literacy experts for students in kindergarten through third grade"– Provided by publisher.
    ISBN 978-1-62617-190-9 (hardcover : alk. paper)
 1. Grizzly bear–Juvenile literature. I. Title.
 QL737.C27B667 2015
 599.784–dc23
                                                                    2014037320

Table of Contents

Grizzly bears are the brown bears of North America. These **mammals** are named for their **grizzled** fur.

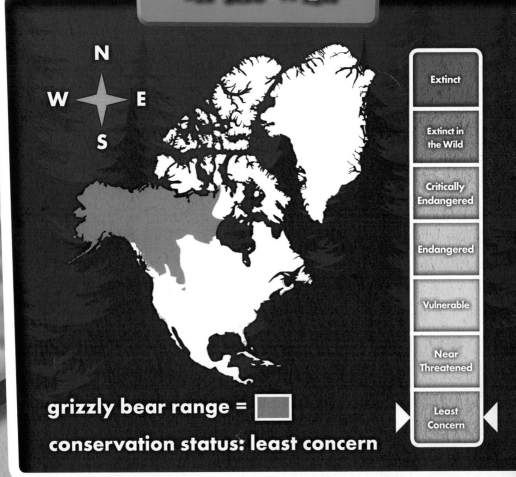

In the Wild

N
W **E**
S

Extinct

Extinct in the Wild

Critically Endangered

Endangered

Vulnerable

Near Threatened

Least Concern

grizzly bear range =

conservation status: least concern

The bears can be found in western Canada and the northwestern United States. They live in forests, **plains**, mountains, and **tundra**.

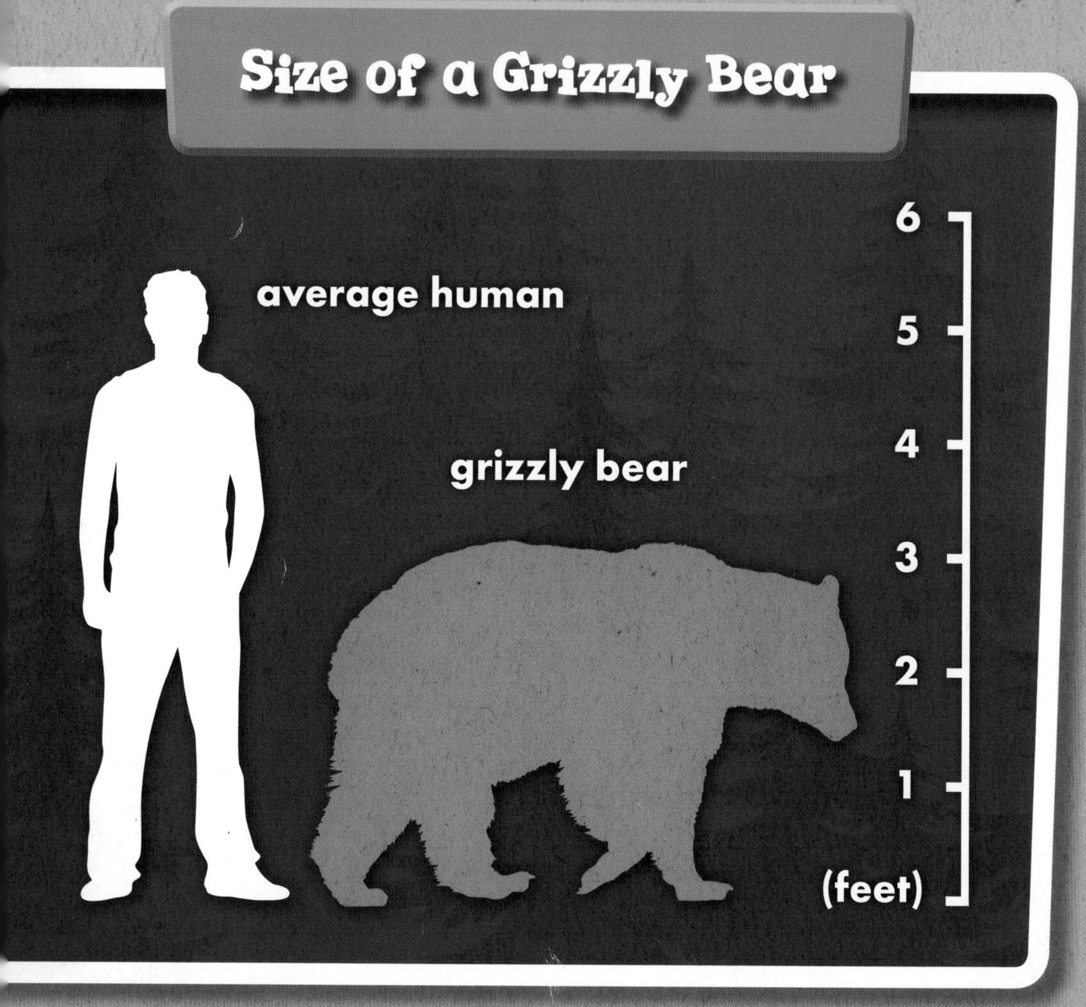
Size of a Grizzly Bear
average human
grizzly bear
6
5
4
3
2
1
(feet)

Grizzly bears are usually bigger than black bears. The largest males measure around 8 feet (2.4 meters) long. Some can weigh more than 1,000 pounds (454 kilograms)!

The bears are very strong.
Between their shoulders is
a large hump of muscles.

Identify a Grizzly Bear

long claws (2 to 4 inches)

short, rounded ears

dish-shaped face

Grizzly bears have long, curved claws for digging. These claws can be 4 inches (10 centimeters) long!

The bears dig in the ground to find food and build **dens**.

An excellent sense of smell leads grizzly bears to food. They **forage** for roots, berries, nuts, and grasses.

dandelions

pine nuts

huckleberries

buffalo berries

grubs

salmon

These **omnivores** also eat **carrion**, insects, and rodents. Sometimes they hunt young moose, elk, and caribou.

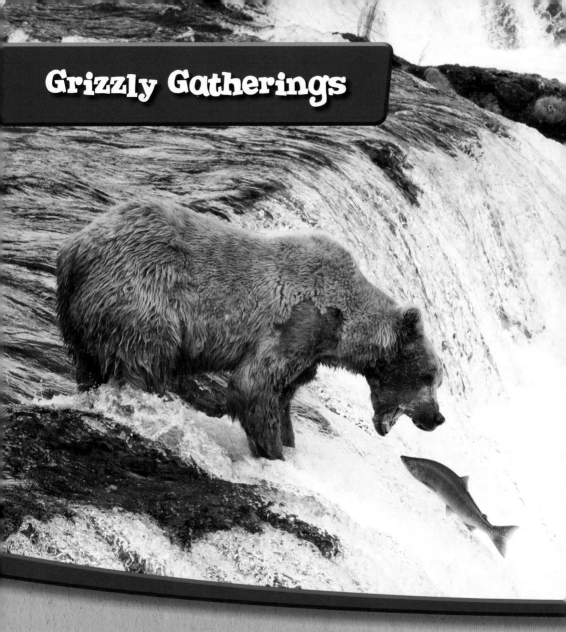

Grizzly bears go to where there is food.

Many gather at Alaskan rivers in summer. They catch jumping salmon in their mouths.

Male grizzly bears also
come together to compete.

They stand on their back legs and wrestle. This is how they fight for females.

15

Grizzly bears eat as much as they can throughout summer and fall.

In late fall, they build their dens.
They stay **dormant** in these
dens during winter.

Bear Cubs

A female gives birth to **cubs** while in her den. The cubs cuddle up to **nurse** and stay warm. In spring, mom and her cubs leave the den.

Baby Facts

Name for babies:	cubs
Size of litter:	2 cubs (most common)
Length of pregnancy:	about 6 to 9 months
Time spent with mom:	about 2 to 3 years

Females protect their young for two to three years.

They look out for wolves, mountain lions, and male grizzly bears. The cubs climb up trees when danger is near!

Glossary

carrion—the rotting meat of a dead animal

cubs—baby grizzly bears

dens—sheltered places; grizzly bears build dens in hillsides, under tree roots, or in rock caves.

dormant—not active

forage—to go out in search of food

grizzled—having white or gray tips

mammals—warm-blooded animals that have backbones and feed their young milk

nurse—to drink mom's milk

omnivores—animals that eat both plants and animals

plains—large areas of flat land

tundra—dry land where the ground is frozen year-round

To Learn More

AT THE LIBRARY

Kolpin, Molly. *Grizzly Bears*. North Mankato, Minn.: Capstone Press, 2013.

Sayre, April Pulley. *Eat Like a Bear*. New York, N.Y.: Henry Holt and Company, 2013.

Stead, Philip Christian. *Bear Has a Story to Tell*. New York, N.Y.: Roaring Brook Press, 2012.

ON THE WEB

Learning more about grizzly bears is as easy as 1, 2, 3.

1. Go to www.factsurfer.com.

2. Enter "grizzly bears" into the search box.

3. Click the "Surf" button and you will see a list of related web sites.

With factsurfer.com, finding more information is just a click away.

Index

The images in this book are reproduced through the courtesy of: Florian Andronache, front cover; Mark Newman/ Getty Images, pp. 4-5; Beck Photography/ Getty Images, p. 7; Richard McManus, p. 8 (top left); Paul Banton, p. 8 (top center); Andrej Stojs, p. 8 (top right); BGSmith, p. 8 (top bottom), pp. 10-11; Paul Souders/ Corbis, pp. 8-9; Melinda Fawver, p. 11 (top left); Pinkcandy, p. 11 (top right); newa, p. 11 (center left); Yuguesh Fagoonee, p. 11 (center right); Vitali Hulai, p. 11 (bottom left); Keith Publicover, p. 11 (bottom right); age fotostock/ SuperStock, pp. 12-13, 16; Richard McManus/ Getty Images, pp. 14-15; Andrea Izzotti, p. 15; Juniors Bildarchiv/ Age Fotostock, p. 17; David Rasmus/ Corbis, pp. 18-19; Radius Images/ Corbis, p. 19; Jrgen & Christine Sohns/ Glow Images, pp. 20-21.